Keeping Records

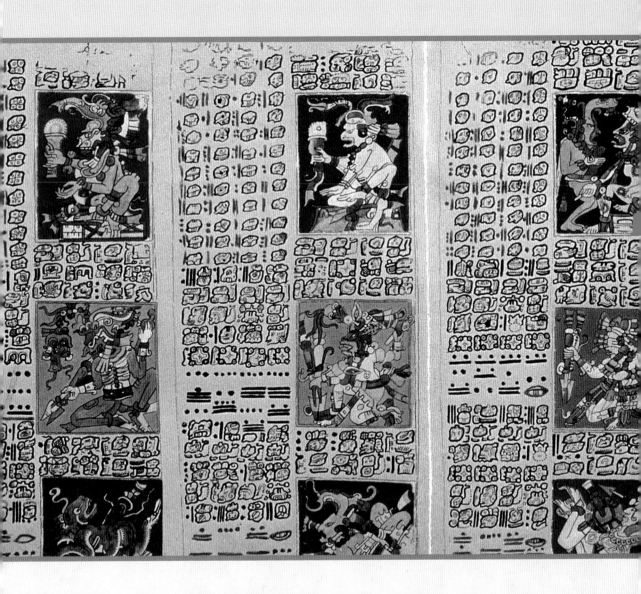

Written by Claire Owen

Mexico

My name is Jorge. I live in Mexico City. I like to learn about number systems from different parts of the world. Why do you think that most people today use a number system that is based on 10?

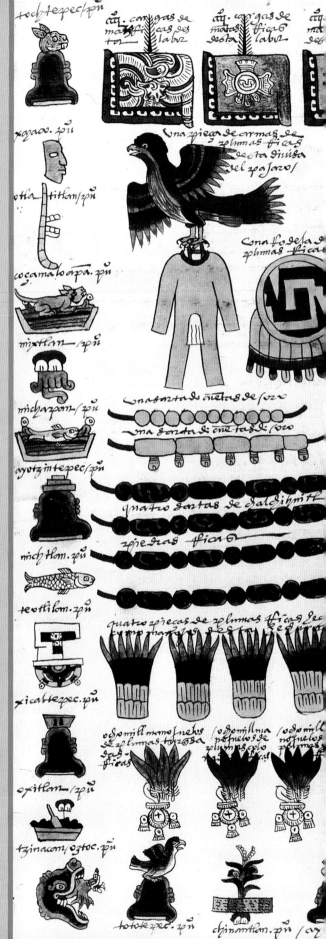

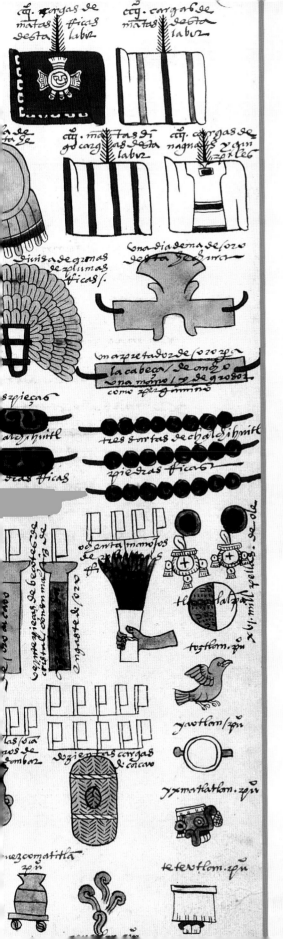

Contents

A New World   4

Ancient Civilizations   6

Maya Numbers   8

Everything in Its Place   10

A Special Number   12

Naming the Days   14

A Circular Calendar   16

The Maya "Century"   18

Aztec Numbers   20

The End of an Empire   22

Sample Answers   24

Index   24

Wherever you see me, you'll find activities to try and questions to answer.

A New World

In 1519, Spanish conquistadors, led by Hernando Cortés, arrived in Mexico in search of Aztec gold. The Aztec empire was centered around the huge city of Tenochtitlan. Farther east lived the Maya people. Both the Aztec and the Maya had developed picture writing, a number system, and calendars that were very different from those used in Europe.

Today, all the Maya cities are in ruins, and many of them have been overgrown by the jungle. Mexico City was built over the ruins of Tenochtitlan.

conquistadors   soldiers who conquered Mexico and Peru in the
                 16th century

Chichen Itza

Uxmal

MAYA

AZTEC EMPIRE

Tikal

Tenochtitlan

How many years ago did Cortés and his men arrive in Mexico?

When the Spanish saw Tenochtitlan, they were amazed. The city, built on an island in a lake, was bigger and more magnificent than any of the cities in Spain.

Ancient Civilizations

The Aztec were a nomadic people who arrived in Mexico around the year 1300. The Maya were a much older people. Their civilization dates back to 2600 B.C. and was at its peak between the years 200 and 900. The Maya used and adapted many of the ideas and customs of another ancient Mesoamerican people, the Olmec.

Even though they did not have metal tools, the Mesoamericans were skilled stone workers. The Olmec carved huge stone heads, up to 11 feet high and weighing up to 40 tons.

Mesoamerica   the region from central Mexico south to the border of Costa Rica, especially before the time of Columbus

Both the Olmec and the Maya played a game with a heavy rubber ball. Players tried to hit the ball through a stone ring set high in the wall—using only their elbows, knees, or hips! The largest Maya ball court measures 545 feet by 232 feet.

A basketball court is 94 feet long and 50 feet wide. How many basketball courts would fit inside the largest Maya ball court?

Maya Numbers

Building on the ideas of the Olmec, the Maya developed a number system based on 20. The symbols they used to record numbers were made up of bars that represented the number five and dots that represented the number one. The Maya used a special symbol for the number zero. The symbol is thought to be a seashell or a closed (empty) fist.

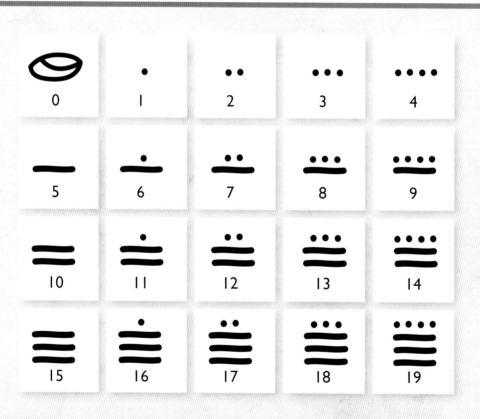

The base-10 number system that we use today has 10 digits: 0, 1, 2, ... 9. The Maya needed 20 "digits" for their base-20 number system.

The Maya "wrote" in pictures on a long, folded strip of bark called a *codex*. Only four of these codices have survived to the present day.

The codex shown here is part of what is known as the Dresden codex. It is the earliest, most beautiful, and best preserved of the Maya codices.

How many of the 20 Maya digits can you find on this page from a Maya codex?

9

Everything in Its Place

In a place-value number system, the value of a digit depends on its place. For example, the digit 2 means two tens in the number 625, but it means two thousands in the number 32,087. The Maya used a place-value system, but their numerals were arranged vertically, with the ones place at the bottom. For example, the value of the places in a four-digit number were—

8,000 (20 x 20 x 20)
400 (20 x 20)
20
1

The Maya number below is equivalent to 18,517.

two 8,000s	2 x 8,000	=	16,000
six 400s	6 x 400	=	2,400
five 20s	5 x 20	=	100
17 ones	17 x 1	=	17
			18,517

equivalent equal in value

A

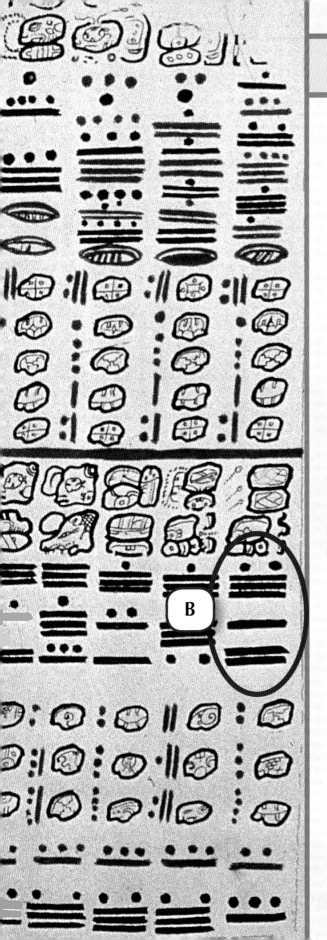

1. Figure out the value of each of these Maya numerals.

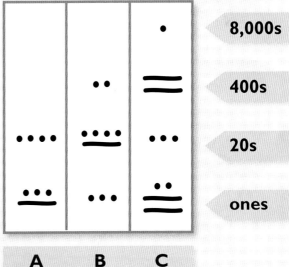

		•	8,000s
	••	━━	400s
••••	••••	•••	20s
•••	•••	••	ones
A	**B**	**C**	

2. Figure out the value of the circled numerals on the codex at the left. (Note that A has 2 digits and B has 3 digits.)

3. Draw dots and lines to show the Maya numeral for each of these numbers:

   a. sixty-five

   b. seventy-one

   c. four hundred sixty-six

A Special Number

In a place-value system, zero acts as a placeholder. Without zero, the numbers 902 and 920, for example, would both look like 92! About 2,300 years ago, the Babylonians began to use their symbol for the number two (𒌋𒌋) on an angle (⟨) to mark an empty place. About 700 years later, the Maya became the first people in the world to think of "nothing" as a number and to create a special symbol for zero.

Look at this detail from a Maya codex. Figure out the value of each of the numerals that includes the symbol for zero.

Maya Number Game

Two players will need a cube with 3 dots and 3 bars, and a cube labeled ones and 20s. (For a greater challenge, use ones, 20s, and 400s on the second cube.)

1. Each player draws boxes for a 2-digit Maya number. (For a greater challenge, draw boxes for a 3-digit number.)

2. Players take turns rolling both cubes and drawing a dot or bar in the appropriate box.

3. Remember that a Maya digit cannot have more than 3 bars and 4 dots.

I've already got 3 bars in the 20s place, so I'll have to miss a turn.

4. After 8 rounds, players figure out their numbers. The player with the greater number scores 1 point.

346. I win!

I got 233.

Play again. The first player with 3 points wins.

Naming the Days

The Maya used two calendars. The *Haab*, or solar calendar, had 365 days. The year was divided into 18 months, each with 20 days, and the "leftover" days formed a special month called *Wayeb*. The first month of the year was *Pohp*, and the first days of the year were *0 Pohp, 1 Pohp*, and so on. After *19 Pohp* came *0 Wo, 1 Wo*, and so on.

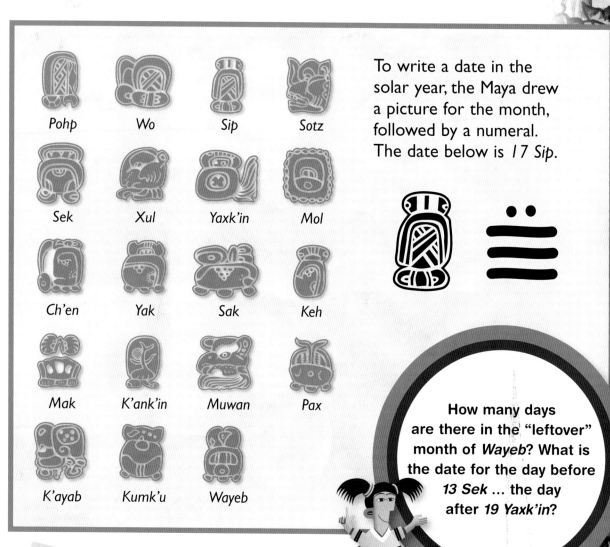

Pohp	Wo	Sip	Sotz
Sek	Xul	Yaxk'in	Mol
Ch'en	Yak	Sak	Keh
Mak	K'ank'in	Muwan	Pax
K'ayab	Kumk'u	Wayeb	

To write a date in the solar year, the Maya drew a picture for the month, followed by a numeral. The date below is *17 Sip*.

How many days are there in the "leftover" month of *Wayeb*? What is the date for the day before *13 Sek* ... the day after *19 Yaxk'in*?

solar   related to the sun

Did You Know?
The Maya thought that the "leftover" days at the end of each year were very unlucky.

Find out how many steps the pyramid at Chichen Itza has altogether. What do you think that number of steps represents?

The Maya built their temples and observatories so that, on certain days of the year, the sun would shine on certain parts of the building.

This famous Maya pyramid at Chichen Itza has 91 steps up each side and one more step around the top level.

A Circular Calendar

The other Maya calendar was the *Tzolkin*, or sacred calendar. This calendar had a cycle of 260 days. It was created by combining 13 numbers with 20 day names, as shown by turning the wheels below. The first day in the cycle was *1 Imix*. Next came *2 Ik*, *3 Ak'bal*, and so on. The 13th day was *13 Ben*, followed by *1 Ix*. In this way, each of the 260 days in the cycle had a **unique** name.

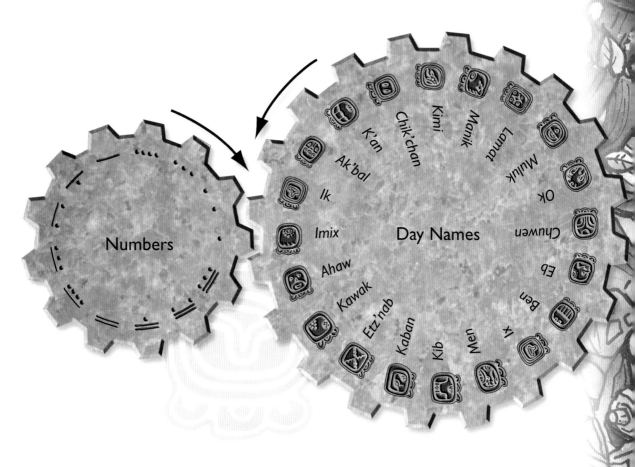

unique   being the only one of its kind

This list shows the first 60 days in the sacred calendar. The Imix days show the start of each new revolution of the larger wheel.

Look at the number pattern in the Imix days: 1, 8, 2, 9, 3, 10. Copy and continue that pattern until you have written 13 numbers in all.

Find and continue a number pattern for the *Kimi* days. What other patterns can you see in the list?

1	Imix	2	Imix	3	Imix
2	Ik	3	Ik	4	Ik
3	Ak'bal	4	Ak'bal	5	Ak'bal
4	K'an	5	K'an	6	K'an
5	Chik'chan	6	Chik'chan	7	Chik'chan
6	Kimi	7	Kimi	8	Kimi
7	Manik	8	Manik	9	Manik
8	Lamat	9	Lamat	10	Lamat
9	Muluk	10	Muluk	11	Muluk
10	Ok	11	Ok	12	Ok
11	Chuwen	12	Chuwen	13	Chuwen
12	Eb	13	Eb	1	Eb
13	Ben	1	Ben	2	Ben
1	Ix	2	Ix	3	Ix
2	Men	3	Men	4	Men
3	Kib	4	Kib	5	Kib
4	Kaban	5	Kaban	6	Kaban
5	Etz'nab	6	Etz'nab	7	Etz'nab
6	Kawak	7	Kawak	8	Kawak
7	Ahaw	8	Ahaw	9	Ahaw
8	**Imix**	**9**	**Imix**	**10**	**Imix**
9	Ik	10	Ik	11	Ik
10	Ak'bal	11	Ak'bal	12	Ak'bal
11	K'an	12	K'an	13	K'an
12	Chik'chan	13	Chik'chan	1	Chik'chan
13	Kimi	1	Kimi	2	Kimi
1	Manik	2	Manik	3	Manik
2	Lamat	3	Lamat	4	Lamat
3	Muluk	4	Muluk	5	Muluk
4	Ok	5	Ok	6	Ok
5	Chuwen	6	Chuwen	7	Chuwen
6	Eb	7	Eb	8	Eb
7	Ben	8	Ben	9	Ben
8	Ix	9	Ix	10	Ix
9	Men	10	Men	11	Men
10	Kib	11	Kib	12	Kib
11	Kaban	12	Kaban	13	Kaban
12	Etz'nab	13	Etz'nab	1	Etz'nab
13	Kawak	1	Kawak	2	Kawak
1	Ahaw	2	Ahaw	3	Ahaw

The Maya "Century"

The Maya used their two calendars together to create a very complicated system of dates. Every day had one of the 260 dates from the sacred calendar and one of the 365 dates from the solar calendar. This system resulted in 18,980 different dates. The first day of the cycle was called *1 Imix 0 Pohp*. This date did not come around again for 52 years!

This carved tablet shows pictures of animals, which represent blocks of time, and pictures of gods, which represent numbers. The date shown, using our calendar, is February 11, 526.

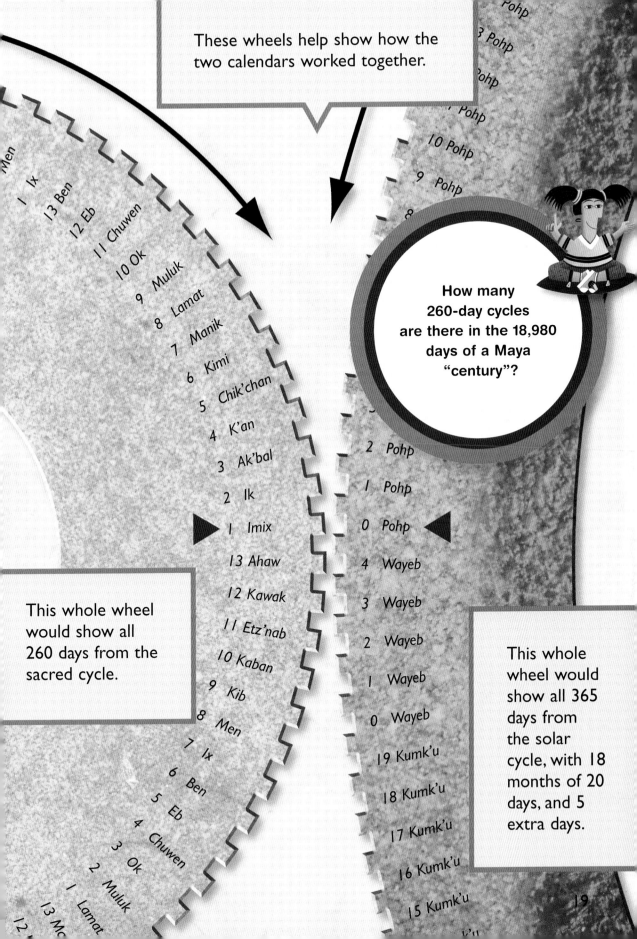

These wheels help show how the two calendars worked together.

How many 260-day cycles are there in the 18,980 days of a Maya "century"?

This whole wheel would show all 260 days from the sacred cycle.

This whole wheel would show all 365 days from the solar cycle, with 18 months of 20 days, and 5 extra days.

Men
1 Ix
13 Ben
12 Eb
11 Chuwen
10 Ok
9 Muluk
8 Lamat
7 Manik
6 Kimi
5 Chik'chan
4 K'an
3 Ak'bal
2 Ik
1 Imix
13 Ahaw
12 Kawak
11 Etz'nab
10 Kaban
9 Kib
8 Men
7 Ix
6 Ben
5 Eb
4 Chuwen
3 Ok
2 Muluk
1 Lamat
13 M
12

3 Pohp
Pohp
Pohp
Pohp
10 Pohp
9 Pohp
8
2 Pohp
1 Pohp
0 Pohp
4 Wayeb
3 Wayeb
2 Wayeb
1 Wayeb
0 Wayeb
19 Kumk'u
18 Kumk'u
17 Kumk'u
16 Kumk'u
15 Kumk'u

Aztec Numbers

The Aztec used a calendar similar to that of the Maya, and they also had a number system based on 20. Although the Aztec had picture symbols for only four numbers, these symbols could be combined or modified to make other numbers. Unlike the Maya number system, this was not a place-value system, because the symbols could be shown in any order.

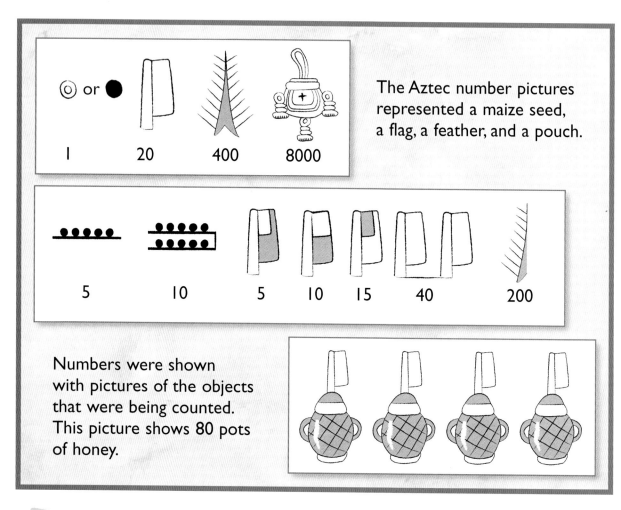

The Aztec number pictures represented a maize seed, a flag, a feather, and a pouch.

⊙ or ●   1
20
400
8000

5   10   5   10   15   40   200

Numbers were shown with pictures of the objects that were being counted. This picture shows 80 pots of honey.

modify   to make changes to

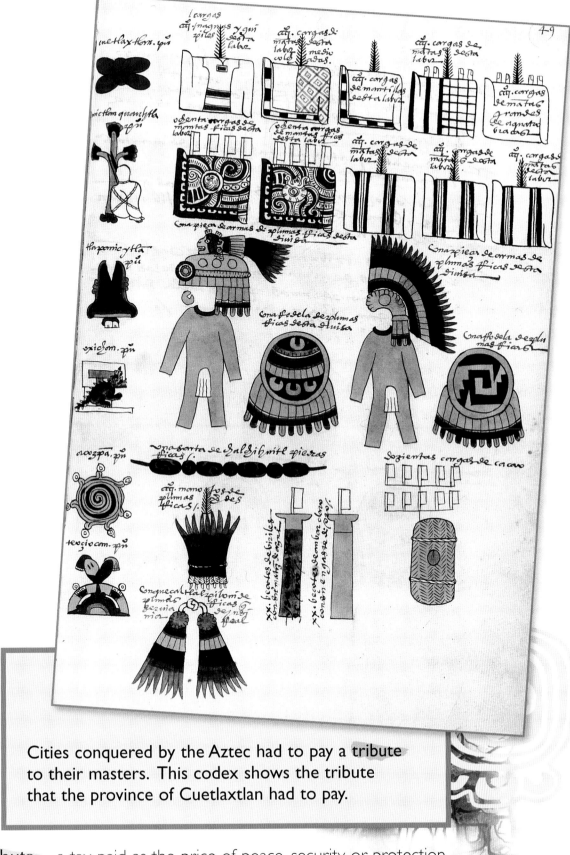

Cities conquered by the Aztec had to pay a tribute
to their masters. This codex shows the tribute
that the province of Cuetlaxtlan had to pay.

tribute   a tax paid as the price of peace, security, or protection

The End of an Empire

Cortés arrived in Mexico with only 500 men and 16 horses, yet he was able to conquer the huge Aztec empire, with its thousands of warriors. According to the Aztec calendar, 1519 was the year in which the god Quetzalcóatl (KET sal KO atl) might return from the east. The Aztec thought that Cortés might be Quetzalcóatl, so they did not attack the Spanish. In this way, the calendar played a part in the downfall of the Aztec.

According to legend, Quetzalcóatl would return on the anniversary of his birthday. These anniversaries occurred once every 52 years. The year 1519 was 572 years after the birth of Quetzalcóatl.

In what year was Quetzalcóatl born? How many 52-year cycles of the calendar were there from his birth year until 1519?

The sun stone, or Aztec "calendar," has become a symbol of Mexico. The original stone was carved in 1479. Weighing nearly 25 tons, it measures almost 12 feet in diameter and is 3 feet thick. Carvings on the stone include the symbols for the months of the year.

Sample Answers

Pretend that you are an Aztec. Draw pictures to show the tribute that you would like to receive. Make sure you use some Aztec numerals in your "codex."

Page 11   1. A: 88   B: 983   C: 12,072
              2. A: 177   B: 6,910
              3. a.   b.   c.

Page 12   900; 1,280; 8

Page 14   5 days; *12 Sek, 0 Mol*

Page 15   365 steps; the days in a year

Page 17   *Imix*: 1, 8, 2, 9, 3, 10, 4, 11, 5, 12, 6, 13, 7

              Kimi: 6, 13, 7, 1, 8, 2, 9, 3, 10, 4, 11, 5, 12

Page 19   73 cycles

Page 23   947; 11 cycles

Index

Aztec codices   21
Aztec number systems   20
calendars   4, 14, 16–20, 22–23
conquistadors   4–5, 22
Maya codices   9, 11–12
Maya number systems   8–12
picture writing   4, 9, 14, 20, 23
Quetzalcóatl   22